Dedications and Th

This book is dedicated to my Mother. She
ceramicist and produced beautiful and interesting works of art throughout her life. My
strength and resilience comes from you mum. I told you I would make you proud.

I would like to thank my family for putting up with me whilst writing this book. Its
been a real labour of love and I have had to learn a lot about how to put a cookbook
together. Dad – thank you for looking after the kids whilst I wrote up my recipes.
Warren – thank you for supporting me when I just needed to do 'one last thing on the
book!'.

Thank you also to my 'new mum cooperative' Louise Desi, who designed the front
cover and illustrated the book, and Rebecca Hughes who helped me with the pictures
and the blog. Thank you both, its been a pleasure working with you on this project.

For every book sold, £1 will be donated to Cancer Research UK. My just giving page
is https://fundraise.cancerresearchuk.org/page/kates-giving-page-291
Copyright © 2018 by Kate S Lewis

FIRST EDITION

Published 2018

Disclaimer

I wanted this book to be made up of recipes that I actually cook on a regular basis. It had to be REAL and it had to be AUTHENTIC. It's not a coffee table cookbook, it's a 'pick me up on a Wednesday evening' cook book, so I encourage you to scribble on it and play about with it.

The pictures were mainly taken on my Iphone and without filters! Some pictures I bought from the internet, as my food tastes yummy but doesn't always look great, so I didn't want to put you off!

I hope you try out as many recipes as you can, and, over time, create your own family favourites and weekly menus.

Kate x

Nom Nom Nom

Over 60 recipes to help you along
the way, from weaning to the family
table

by kate lewis

Contents

Introduction

I'm Kate Lewis, mum to two boys Ben and Noah. I used to run a Pilates studio and would often talk to clients about the benefits of healthy eating. I have a real passion for home cooking, making delicious meals using the freshest ingredients and keeping it organic and seasonal.

I started to write this book, simply as a means of keeping track of my favourite recipes and I thought some of you might find it useful.

Once the single flavour puree stage was over, I wanted good, hearty meals, that I could prepare when the little ones went down for their afternoon nap. I could then heat up for dinner or lunch the next day.

Some meals went straight on the floor, but I persevered, and generally they grew to love them. Now they eat just about anything I put infront of them 'hashtag proud mummy' :)

My philosophy when it comes to cooking is that we should enjoy our food as well as it benefit our health. I hope you enjoy making these recipes as much as I have enjoyed putting them together. Most of the recipes are for the whole family as I am a firm believer in the whole family eating the same food.

As I continue to add to this book I hope you will continue to use it as a resource for flavoursome family meals...enjoy!

Top 10 Tips For Creating An Adventurous Little Eater

1. Try to create a foodie home. Let your kids see you prepare food. Let them watch whilst you butter the bread, cut the avocado, slice the watermelon. Do as much as you can in front of them. They will then see you enjoying the preparation of food and it will add to the excitement of eating a meal. Even in the puree phase let them see as much as they can.

2. Let them play with whole foods, apples, oranges, any veg. Let them feel the food as much as possible.

3. Once they are able to hold and pick up the food, let them eat with their hands. Try not to spoon feed too much. Let your baby feel the texture of the food and smell the food. They might start to move the food about and separate the food (some babies don't like their food being mixed up), let this happen. Its only in an adult world that we have to just bring the food from the plate to our mouths.

4. Let them get messy;) Every ounce of you will be screaming inside thinking, 'I have slaved over this meal and you just rub your face in it', not to mention the cleaning up. But just take a breath, relax, keep things light hearted and the dining table a pleasant environment.

5. The following rule is one of the most important rules that I live by and I would encourage you to adopt. Try not to talk about your babies food habits in front of them. You know how you love the fact that they understand more than you think? Well, they understand more than you think! Remember nothing is binary in their little world, what they don't like today will probably become their favourite food next week. Please refrain from talking in social groups about your kids eating habits, and try not to comment on other kids eating habits, however trivial they are. If you have particular worries, talk to your GP.

6. As I have said, babies will change their mind, nothing is set in stone. One day they love bananas the next day they spit them out. Do not worry – just go with it. Leave the banana for a couple of days and try again. Don't presume anything – this only creates an environment where everyone is anxious. Just put the food down and look away.

7. At about 10 months (although it can happen at any time) they can go through a difficult spurt where they are starting to learn cause and effect. This can lead to your baby simply throwing their food on the floor, at the walls, at the dog! They are working out that if they do this, that will happen. Its just a phase and stage.

8. Only give them two snacks per day and if possible even the snacks should be eaten sitting down at a table. They must learn that the table is a place of intrigue, nice things happen at the dinner table. Refrain from too many snacks, although make sure the snacks are low GI and whole food snacks, don't let your little one munch away on rice cakes (which have little to no nutritional value in them) between meals.

9. Try not to substitute foods. If he doesn't eat a meal its not the end of the world. Wait until the next meal and he will hopefully eat that. If he misses dinner it will just mean he will be hungry for breakfast the next morning. If you are trying something new for dinner, try to have a fantastic day of play and fresh air, talk about things that you have been up to whilst making the dinner and create a happy environment.

10. Eat what your kids eat. You must have integrity in what you say. There is no point in serving up a plate of steamed broccoli and expecting them to eat it when you are about to munch away on a take out. Eat the same snacks. Drink water like they do. Make food you love, add bundles of flavour, and your kids will love it just like their parents do.

KITCHEN ESSENTIALS

The following list is a compilation of 'store cupboard essentials'. Generally if you have, at least, these ingredients in the house you can whip up a quick meal. This list is obviously not exclusive and you will no doubt have things to add or take out but generally I find that its at least a good start to help you come up with the weekly menu.

☐ Eggs
☐ Olive or vegetable oil
☐ Oats
☐ Unsalted butter
☐ Bicarb of soda
☐ Baking powder
☐ Plain flour
☐ Onion
☐ Garlic
☐ Pasta
☐ Avocado
☐ Can of chopped tomatoes
☐ Can of tuna
☐ Can of sardines
☐ Rice
☐ Couscous
☐ Curry powder
☐ Spices, cumin, coriander, turmeric, garam masala
☐ Potatoes
☐ Fruit
☐ Live natural yoghurt

FOR THE FREEZER
(great if you run out of the essentials or want to whip up an Omlette or quick pasta)

☐ Chopped onion/shallot
☐ Chopped garlic
☐ Ginger
☐ Herbs like parsley, coriander, basil etc
☐ Spinach
☐ Mushrooms
☐ Frozen peas

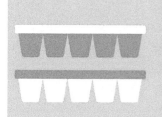

MEASURING CUPS

Buy yourself some measuring cups. They can often be easier then using weighing scales and you don't have to guess how much a cup is.

ICE CUBE TRAY

Large ice cube trays are an ideal way of portioning out your pureed foods. Simply take out one or two cubes and let them defrost in the fridge, ready to heat them up the following day.

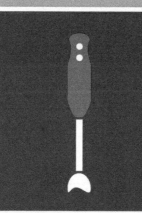

HAND HELD BLENDER

The hand held blender is going to be your friend for at least the next few months, especially when pureeing. Keep her safe and warm!

METAL STEAMER

I like to steam my veg as it keeps as much of the nutritional value in it as possible, but you could boil. The metal steamer is great and doesn't take up too much room.

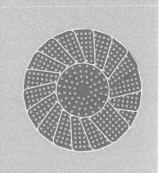

KITCHEN SCALES

I sometimes swap between cups and mls when cooking. The weighing scales are good for mixing up lots of ingredients at once.

MUFFIN & LOAF TINS

The muffin tin and loaf tin you will need for... the muffin and loaf recipes! Get them now before you make the mix and then have nothing to bake them in. I have done that before!

PURÉES

In the first month or so of weaning simply offer your child a different puree at each mealtime. Keep the flavours varied so it's not only sweet puree at the start.

Vary the textures of your purees as soon as possible so they get used to lumpy and textured food during early weaning.

Avocado Purée

1/2 Avocado
Lemon juice

METHOD

1. Cut the avocado in half by tracing the skin lengthways with a knife and twisting it to separate
2. Then scoop out the flesh of the avocado with a spoon and mash it up with a fork
3. Add a few drops of lemon juice to keep the avocado fresh.

Banana Purée

INGREDIENTS

1 medium banana
1 or 2 Pabst baby's usual milk

METHOD

1. Peel the banana and cut it in half
2. Using a fork mash one half of the banana adding the milk if required to get the desired consistency.
3. Keep the other half and serve for
   baby led weaning. Your baby will like to just hold the banana in
her hand whilst you are feeding the purée.

NOTE: Any remaining banana can be kept for 24 hours in an airtight container in the fridge.

Butternut Purée

1/2 Butternut squash
1 or 2 tbsp baby's usual milk

METHOD

1. Peel the butternut with a knife carefully, slicing down the length of the butternut with a knife, also de-seed.
2. Cut it into cubes roughly and boil or steam for about 7 minutes.
3. Then place in a food processor with the milk and blitz until smooth. Add more milk or water if desired.

Carrot & Apple Purée

INGREDIENTS

1 large carrot, peeled and cut into rounds
1 whole apple, peeled and cut into quarters
1 clove

METHOD

1. Steam the carrot and apple in a steamer until soft. Take out the clove.
2. Then blend with a splash of water or babies milk to desired consistency.

Beetroot & Sweet Potato Purée

INGREDIENTS

1 whole raw beetroot- diced
1 medium sweet potato
1 tbsp. of vegetable oil

METHOD

1. Peel and cut the sweet potato into cubes
2. Place in a pan of boiling water and cook for 5-6 minutes
3. Add the diced beetroot and cook for a further 5 minutes
4. Remove from the heat, drain and then add the oil.
5. Blitz in a blender until smooth

Broccoli Purée

INGREDIENTS

1 half a broccoli
1 or 2 tbsp baby's usual milk
Extra water

METHOD

1. Chop up the broccoli into small pieces
2. Boil or steam the broccoli until tender (do not over cook)
3. Purée most of the broccoli with a little milk and keep a couple of florets to told and play with whilst you feed the purée.

Fish & Pea Purée

1 fillet of skinless, boneless firm white fish (e.g. hake, cod, sea bream)
1/2 cup frozen peas
3 tbsp baby's usual milk
1 tsp butter

METHOD

1. Place the fish in a pan with the milk and cover. Cook the fish on a low heat for about 6-7 mins. Add the butter just at the last minute.
2. In a separate pan cook the peas for about 4 mins.
3. Once the fish and peas are cooked blitz them up in a food processor or using a hand held blender until smooth. Add some of the pea water to loosen the mixture if desired.

Fish, Sweet Potato & Cheese Purée

INGREDIENTS

1 sweet potato, peeled and chopped into cubes
A knob of butter
100ml baby's usual milk
50g cheddar cheese
200g soft white fish
1 bay leaf

METHOD

1. Boil the sweet potato for about 6-7 mins.
2. Place the fish in a saucepan with the milk and bay leaf and poach the fish for about 5-6 mins or until it flakes easily.
3. Strain the milk but keep it to one side. Discard the bay leaf.
4. Put the fish and potato in a food processor with butter and cheese and blitz to form a purée.

Carrot Purée & Carrot Sticks

INGREDIENTS

2 medium carrots
2 tbsp baby's usual milk or
water

METHOD

1. Chop the carrots into small pieces.
2. Steam (or boil) the carrots for around 6-7 mins or until al-dente.
3. Drain the carrots and pop them in a food processor or you can use a hand blender.
4. Add 2 tbsp baby's usual milk and blend until smooth

Fish & Butternut Purée

INGREDIENTS

1 fillet of white fish, skinned
1 half butternut squash, peeled and chopped
2-3 tbsp baby's usual milk

METHOD

1. Poach the fish in a pan with the milk. Cook till the fish flakes easily.
2. Boil the butternut until cooked and place all the ingredients in the food processor. Blitz until smooth.

Note: This purée is a great way to introduce fish into your babies diet. The butternut gives it a creaminess and therefore not too 'fishy'.

Pea Purée

100g frozen peas
2 tbsp baby's usual milk

METHOD

1. Place the peas in boiling water for 3-4 mins.
2. Drain the peas and pop into a food processor or a hand held blender.
3. Add about 2tbsp of your baby's usual milk and blitz until smooth.

Pear Purée

INGREDIENTS

1 ripe pear, peeled and cut into cubes
2 tbsp baby's usual milk

METHOD

1. Place the pear in a saucepan with just enough water to cover it.
2. Bring to the boil and simmer for 2 to 3 mins. Drain and return to a bowl
3. Add about 2tbsp of your baby's usual milk and blitz until desired consistency.

NOTE:
Add a clove to the pear when cooking then discard before you blend. This might help with teething pain.

Potato, Leek & Pea Purée

INGREDIENTS

1 medium potato
1/2 small leek
1/2 cup peas

METHOD

1. Boil or steam the potatoes.
2. Whilst you do this, in a frying pan, add a splash of oil and fry off the leeks.
3. Steam the peas.
4. Once all parts are cooked, mix them together and place in a blender and blitz until smooth. Add a splash of milk if desired.

Simple Cauliflower Purée

INGREDIENTS

100g frozen cauliflower florets
2 tbsp baby's usual milk

METHOD

1. Boil the cauliflower florets for about 7 mins or until soft.
2. Drain and pop in a food processor.
3. Add 1 or 2 tbsp of milk.

Note: Don't over boil the cauliflower (if it feels soft, remove it from the boiling water).

Sweet Potato Purée

1 medium sweet potato, washed and peeled
1 - 2 tsp unsalted butter

METHOD

1. Cut up the sweet potato and boil until soft.
2. Drain and add the butter.
3. Purée until smooth or desired consistency.

BREAKFASTS

These breakfasts are all relatively low Glycemic Index.

They are designed to keep you fuller for longer and so they are a great alternative to the, frankly, dire selection of 'flavoured air' we call breakfast cereal.

You could use most of these recipes as mid morning or mid afternoon snacks.

This is the most important meal of the day – make it wholesome, make it fibrous and make it count!

Bircher Muesli

This is so easy to make and this recipe takes rolled oats to the next level. A staple in our household, this can be made in advance and kept in the fridge for up to 3 days. Breakfast ready prepared for the next day - fabulous!

Serves 4
Prep Time 10 minutes. Leave it for at least 30 mins so that the oats can soak up all the liquid.

INGREDIENTS

1 cup Rolled oats
1 cup Natural bio-live Yoghurt
1 cup apple juice
Pinch of Cinnamon
1 apple – grated

METHOD

1. Put all the ingredients into a large bowl and mix together.

2. Add more apple juice or yoghurt to make it wet if you desire.

Note: You can add whatever you like to this recipe, like the picture, add fruit, chopped nuts, linseeds, dates, oat bran, nutmeg.

Blueberry Pancakes (no sugar)

Healthy, flavoursome blueberry pancakes. Very simple and can be made with fresh or frozen berries.

Serves: 4
Prep Time: 15 minutes – Cooking Time: 20 minutes

INGREDIENTS

90g rolled oats
1tsp baking powder
150ml Greek yoghurt
1 banana
2 eggs
3 drops of vanilla extract (optional)
Splash of milk
Butter, for greasing
Small punnet of blueberries – fresh or frozen

METHOD

1. Place the oats, baking powder, yoghurt, banana, eggs and vanilla extract into a blender and blitz until smooth. Add a splash of milk if the mixture appears too thick (it should resemble double cream). Let the mixture sit for a few minutes to thicken slightly.

2. Grease a large non-stick pan with butter and heat over a medium-low heat. Use your judgement to decide how many pancakes to do at any one time.

3. Using an ice-cream scoop or similar, drop some of the batter into the pan and put a few blueberries on top.

4. Cook until bubbles appear on top of the pancake. Flip over the pancake and cook until golden brown.
    Then transfer to a plate, wipe the pan clean and start again until all the mixture is used up. Serve these with some natural yoghurt or on their own, slightly warm.

Natural Yoghurt with Chia Seeds & Berry Compote

The chai seeds in this recipe give the berries a thicker consistancy.

Serves: 1 - Simply double or treble the quantities to make more.
Prep Time: 5

INGREDIENTS

3 tbsp natural yoghurt
1 tsp chia seeds
1 tbsp frozen berries

METHOD

1, Simply mix 1 tsp of chia seeds with about 3 tbsp of natural
    yoghurt.

2. To make berry compote simply defrost 1 tbsp of frozen
    berries and mix in with the yoghurt. The chai seeds will make
    the mixture a little glutenous, so turning the berries into a jam like
    consistancy.

Cheese, shallot and Turmeric Omelettes

This recipe was taken from a fabulous book called 'Flavour Led Weaning' by Zainab Jagot Ahmed. Adding a little turmeric to the omelette is a great way of introducing a new flavour and a new spice to your babies diet.

Serves: 1
Prep Time: 10 minutes – Cooking Time: 10 minutes

INGREDIENTS

1 tbsp Olive oil
A small handful of frozen
shallots
1 egg
1 tsp whole milk
Pinch of black pepper
Pinch of ground turmeric
A small handful of Medium
cheddar cheese - grated

METHOD

1. Heat the oil in a medium non-stick frying pan on a low-medium heat.

2. Add the shallots and sauté for 2 mins until soft.
    the onion is cooking, crack the egg into a bowl and add the cheese, milk, black pepper and turmeric and whisk to combine. Then reduce the heat to low and spread the onions around the pan.

3. Add the egg mixture to the pan and tilt the pan so that the mixture covers the base evenly. Gently cook the egg on one side until brown then flip it over to cook the other side. If you have trouble flipping the omelette you could fold it in half and then cook it until the egg is cooked through.

4. Then remove from the pan and cut into bite size pieces. Serve with avocado and cherry tomatoes.

Low GI Granola

This is such a flavoursome and nutritious breakfast. I use Agave syrup which is a low glycemic index sweetener and completely natural. It comes straight from the Agave plant in Mexico.

You could put this in an airtight glass jar and nibble at it throughout the day. The kids could have it in their yoghurt, it could be sprinkled on their breakfast or porridge, or they can eat it as it is.

Prep: 10 mins Cook: 20 mins

INGREDIENTS
240g oats
120g mixed nuts – ground down
120g seeds – also ground down
Small handful of raisins
Small handful of desiccated coconut
120g of coconut oil
60g agave syrup

METHOD

1. Preheat the oven to 180/160 fan.

2. Put all the ingredients in a bowl and mix with your hands until it's all mixed together.

3.   Line a flat shallow tray with parchment/baking paper and spread the mixture over it evenly.

4. Bake in the oven for 20 mins, stirring half way through to ensure it does not burn and that all the mixture is cooked evenly.

5. Let it cool before you enjoy!

33

Porridge Oat Flapjacks

This Cow & Gate recipe makes amazingly simple porridge oat flapjacks

Serves: about 5 flapjacks

1 cup of porridge oats
1.5 cups of whole milk or
breast milk
1 banana

1. Put the oven onto 180C/160 fan or gas mark 6.

2. Place the oats and the milk in a mixing bowl and combine to make dough.

3. Add the banana and mash it up with a fork then mix it all so that the banana combines with the oats.

4. Grease a loaf tin. Then place the mixture into the tin and pat down.

5. Cook on the middle shelf for 15-20 mins or until it turns a light brown on top.

6. Let it cool and cut into 1inch wide finger shapes.

Stewed Apple with Nutmeg & Clove

This is a warming and family friendly breakfast recipe. Try it on its own or with natural yoghurt and my home made Granola. It also opens the bowels beautifully!

Serves: 4
Prep Time: 10 – Cooking Time: 15

INGREDIENTS

1 cooking apple or Granny Smith apple
Pinch of nutmeg
1 whole clove

METHOD

1. Peel the apple and cut into small pieces.

2. Place the apple in a pan with just enough water to cover the apple. About 2 or 3 tbsps.

3. Add the clove and nutmeg. Cook until the apple is soft.

LUNCH

Lunches can be tricky. We are usually out or have just rushed back home. I usually make the lunches on the back of making dinner and we can have it the next day. However, in the absence of leftovers for lunch I have added recipes that are quick to prepare and can be kept in the fridge and eaten on for a few days.

As with breakfast, make time for lunch, don't over feed on snacks. Get them used to the routine of breakfast – snack – lunch – snack – dinner.

Annabel's Vegetable Rissoles

This recipe was taken from Annabel Carmel. They are easy to make and a great snack or light lunch. Try to serve them warm.

Makes 10-12
Prep: 10 mins Cook: 10 mins

INGREDIENTS

1 large sweet potato – peeled and chopped
1/2 a butternut squash
150g potato – peeled
75g leeks – white part only, washed and finely chopped
150g mushrooms – chopped
2 tbsp chopped parsley (frozen chopped parsley is fine)

125g fresh breadcrumbs
1/2 tbsp low salt soy sauce
1/2 lightly beaten egg
Ground pepper to season
Plain flour for coating
Vegetable oil for frying

METHOD

1. Grate the sweet potato, potato and squash. Squeeze out some of the excess moisture from the pulp.

2. In a mixing bowl, combine all vegetables with the parsley, breadcrumbs, soy sauce and beaten egg.

3. Form the mixture into about 12 golf sized balls then lightly toss in flour

4. Heat the oil in a pan. Add the rissoles a few at a time, depending on the size of your pan. Cook for about 8-10 minutes, turning occasionally. Serve as a light lunch with avocado or cherry tomatoes.

Beetroot Hummus

The beetroot is high in Vitamin C, and the chickpeas are a great source of protein. Try this with my cheesy oatcakes (p.g 42)

Prep Time: 10 – Cooking Time: 15

INGREDIENTS

1 x 400g can of chickpeas – drained and rinsed
250g cooked beetroot
Juice of half a lemon
1 clove of garlic – crushed
2 tbsp tahini (omit this for babies under 12 months)
2 tsp ground cumin
100ml extra virgin olive oil
Finely chopped parsley to garnish

METHOD

Place all of the ingredients into a food processor and blitz until smooth.

That's it...! I have no further instructions :)

Note: Cooked beetroot can be found in the vegetable isle of the supermarket. It usually comes vacuum packed. Make sure its not the picketed beetroot you are buying.

Cheesy Oatcakes

These cheesy oatcakes are much more moist than the ones you buy at the supermarket. More substantial also.

Serves: 6-8
Prep Time 15 minutes – Cooking Time: 20-25

INGREDIENTS

1 cup of rolled oats
1/2 cup buckwheat flour
80ml of light olive oil
Dash of hot water
50g mature, medium or mild
cheddar (as you prefer)

METHOD

1. Preheat oven to 180c and line baking tray with greaseproof paper.

2. Add oats, water, oil and cheese to large mixing bowl and combine to make a dough.

3. Set aside for 15 minutes to allow water to absorb.

4. Dust a clean worktop with flour and roll out the dough to about 3mm thick.

5. Using a cutter or a cup or alike cut out the oat cakes and place them on the baking tray.

6. Bake for about 20-25 minutes or until golden brown.

43

Home-made Sweet Potato Wedges

Super simple - call them chips :) You could offer these as a snack (once cooked, gently heat them in a microwave) or serve with meat or fish for a wholesome dinner. By keeping the potato skin on your baby will get the fibre and roughage, although they may pick it off as time goes on ;)

Prep: 5 mins Cook: 30 mins
INGREDIENTS

1 large sweet potato
1 tbsp of vegetable oil
Pepper to season
Or try a sprinkle of paprika if
your little one is ready

METHOD

1. Chop the sweet potato in half, length ways then again and again to make wedges.

2. Place on a baking tray and add the oil and pepper.

3. Bake for around 30 mins but check with a fork before serving.

Hummus

INGREDIENTs

300g carton of chickpeas - drained
115g Tahini
Olive oil to taste
Lemon juice to taste
1 garlic clove crushed

METHOD

1. In a food processor add the chickpeas and tahini and blitz.

2. Add the olive oil and lemon juice to taste then add the crushed garlic. Blitz until smooth.

Fish Cakes

It can be difficult to get your little one to eat fish, especially if, as a family, you don't eat it much. These fish cakes make a yummy lunch or dinner and its a sneaky way of getting fish into their diets more easily.

Serves: 8-10 fish cakes
Prep: 15 mins Cook: 10 mins

INGREDIENTS

Two fillets of firm white fish
like haddock, hake or cod
1 egg
Roughly half a cup of
breadcrumbs (you can buy these)
1 tbsp oil
1 tbsp capers roughly chopped
Three spring onions chopped finely
1 or two garlic cloves crushed
1 medium tomato chopped finely
Pepper to season

METHOD

1. Chop up the fish roughly but finely, then place it in a mixing bowl together with all the other ingredients. Mix it together with your hands.

2. Heat the oil in a frying pan over a medium heat.

3. Scoop up a golf ball sized amount of mixture into your hands and shape to make patties. Repeat until the mixture is used up.

4, Place patties in the pan, a few at a time in the pan, Cook the fish cakes for 6-7 mins turning once or twice with a spatula or tongs. They should be golden brown.

5. Place them on kitchen towel to soak up the excess oil.

6. Serve warm or at room temperature with chopped up avocado or cherry tomatoes. They make wonderful finger food.

Flour & Yoghurt Flat breads

Making bread has never been so easy. These flat breads have just three ingredients in them and are so easy.

Serves: 12 small portions
Prep: 15 mins Cook: 20-25 mins

INGREDIENTS

500g Plain Flour
500ml Bio live yoghurt – natural
1 tbsp baking powder

METHOD

1. Turn on the oven to 180c/160 fan or gas mark 6.

2. Place all three ingredients into a large mixing bowl and mix with your hands for about 3-4 mins. The mixture will be slightly more wet than a normal bread dough although if it seems too wet add a little more flour.

3. Place greaseproof paper on to a large baking tray and separate the mixture into about 10-12 balls and flatten into small pita bread shapes.

4. Place the breads into the middle shelf of the oven for 20-25 mins.

Gail's Sweetcorn Fritters

Aunty Gail is a superb cook, and she makes the most amazing sweetcorn fritters. This was one of the first recipes I tried out once the children were born. They are a great alternative to the sandwich and have just the right amount of 'cooking processes in there to whet your appetite for baking.

Serves: 8 Fritters
Prep: 20 mins Cook: 10 mins

INGREDIENTS

2 eggs beaten
500ml buttermilk (if you want to make your own buttermilk, 1tbsp lemon juice to 250ml full fat milk. Let stand for
10 mins)
1/2 tsp bicarbonate of soda
2 tsp baking powder
1/2 tsp salt
1 cup brown or plain flour
1/2 cup oats

2 cups frozen sweetcorn
1 tbsp coriander, chopped finely (you can use frozen herbs)
1 tbsp vegetable oil

METHOD

1. Mix all ingredients together in a mixing bowl.

2. Heat the oil in a frying pan.

3. Using an ice cream scoop or similar place two or three scoops (depending on the size of your pan) of the mixture into the pan and cook on a low/medium heat until golden brown. Turning once. Repeat until all the mixture is used up.

4. Serve with yoghurt and avocado or a poached egg

Fresh Pesto & Crushed Pine Nuts

This pesto is much lower in salt and just tastes fresher.
It keeps well in the fridge for about 2/3 days in an airtight container.

Prep: 10 mins Cook: 12 mins (for the pasta)

INGREDIENTS

1 cup of basil
1 cup of baby leaf spinach
1/2 cup of freshly grated Parmesan cheese
1/2cup extra virgin olive oil
1/3 cup pine nuts
3 garlic cloves – minced
Freshly ground black pepper

METHOD

1. Place all the ingredients in a food processor and blitz until desired consistency.

2. Serve with fresh pasta and a sprinkle of olive oil. Add crushed pine nuts as a garnish if you like.

Gemma's Porridge Oat Loaf

My friend Gemma makes the best porridge oat loaf, this recipe had to be included in my book.

Serves: 1 loaf
Prep Time: 20 minutes – Cooking Time: 30 minutes

INGREDIENTS

2 cups porridge oats
4 cups natural bio live yoghurt
2 tbsp chia seeds
1 grated apple
Handful of raisins
½ tsp cinnamon
½ tsp baking powder

METHOD

1. Turn on the oven to 180c/160c fan/gas mark 6.

2. Mix the oats and yoghurt together with your hands.

3. Then add the grated apple and chai seeds and continue to mix.

4. Add the remainder of the ingredients.

5. Place in to a loaf tin and cook for 25-30 mins

Variations:
Although I made this oatmeal loaf with dried fruit and apple you could add whatever you like to be honest.

Try adding mixed seeds, blueberries, dried dates or figs, carrot, cranberry or even a savoury version with garlic and chilli.

Whatever you have in the house, give it a go!

Falafel with Yoghurt Dip

These little falafel balls are full of goodness. Served with natural runny yoghurt and avocado and slightly warm, they are a lovely lunch or even an on-the-go snack on their own.

Serves: 6
Prep Time: 15 mins – Cooking Time: 15 mins

INGREDIENTS

400g canned chick peas –drained
1 tsp ground cumin
1 tbsp fresh coriander (frozen is fine)
1 garlic cloves, crushed
Groundnut/sunflower oil for frying –
or any oil with a high burn tolerance
Natural yoghurt to serve

METHOD

1. Place all the ingredients except the yoghurt and the oil in a food processor and blitz coarsely.

2. Divide into about 12 balls. Heat the oil in a non-stick frying pan and cook the balls for about 6 minutes or until golden. You will probably have to do a few at a time depending on the size of your pan.

3. Serve with yoghurt and lightly toasted pita bread with butter.

Gluten Free Pizza

Another alternative to bread. you can get creative with this one and for older kids – if you call it a pizza, its a pizza!

Serves: 1 pizza
Prep: 5 mins Cook: 30 mins

INGREDIENTS

2 eggs
1 cup grated cheese
1 tsp oregano

Topping:
1 tbsp tomato purée
Your choice of chopped onion,
feta cheese, sliced tomato,
chopped ham, sweet peppers,
sliced mushroom etc.

METHOD

1. Preheat the oven to 180, 160 fan, gas mark 4. Line a baking tray with a non-stick baking sheet.

2. To prepare the base, combine the eggs, cheese and oregano. Pour the mixture onto the prepared baking tray. Bake in the oven for about 30 mins or until the base is golden and crisp.

3. Spread the tomato purée evenly over the pizza base then add the toppings of your choice. Bake the pizza again for 15 mins or until the cheese has melted. Once cooked, garnish with ingredients of your choice.

Onion Bahji

These onion bahji's are great as a light lunch for the whole family or wrap them in foil and take them out as a snack. They are moist enough for be eaten without any dip or sauce and, as they are made with gram flour, they are gluten free!

Makes about 10

INGREDIENTS

Oil for frying
2 white onions
100g gram flour
2 cloves garlic
1/2 tsp ginger (use the frozen kind if you like)
1/2 tsp turmeric
1/2 tsp cumin
1/2 tsp garam masala

METHOD

1. Using a Mandolin, slice the onions – not too finely, I usually use the thick slice option. Or you can slice manually.

2. Dust a little flour into the onions to separate them.

3. Then in a large mixing bowl add the dry ingredients.

4. Then add the onions to the mixing bowl and mix together with your hands.

5. Add a little oil to a large frying pan. Then pick up a small handful of the onion mixture and form into a patty. Add to the pan, a few at a time, and cook for a few minutes each side. They should be golden brown.

6. Once cooked, transfer to a plate covered with kitchen towel to soak up excess oil. Serve with yoghurt and grated cucumber mixed up.

Savoury Muffins

Not actually a muffin, more like a baked omlette but an easy light lunch for the family again and no bread!
Serve with sliced up cherry tomatoe and avocado and maybe a savoury oat cake on the side.

Makes about 8-10 muffins
Prep time: 10 mins Cooking time: 30 mins

INGREDIENTS

1 tbsp of chopped shallots (use
the frozen ready chopped)
Small knob of butter
4 eggs
3 broccoli florets chopped up
small
1 tbsp crème fraiche
2 tbsp. grated cheese
1 tsp baking powder
50 ml cream
Pinch of black pepper

METHOD

1. Preheat the oven to 170C grease the pan. Use small muffin pan or cupcake pan.

2. Fry the onion on a small knob of butter.

3. Combine the rest of the ingredients into a bowl, except for the broccoli. That needs to mix in with the onion.
4. Combine both mixtures. Then pour the batter into the muffin cups and bake for about 30 mins.

Yummy Potato Cakes

Great alternative to sandwiches for lunch and they keep well in the fridge.

Prep: 15 mins Cook: 10 mins

INGREDIENTS

1 bag of new potatoes – peeled
and cut into large chunks
1 tsp fenugreek seeds
3 tbsp olive oil
1 bunch salad onions – trimmed
and finely chopped
2 garlic cloves crushed
1 tsp turmeric
1 pack of fresh coriander
2 tbsp flour

METHOD

1. Boil the potatoes for about 12-15 mins until cooked through.

2. Drain the potatoes and return to the saucepan.

3. Place the fenugreek seeds in a large frying pan and toast over a low heat for a couple of mins. Then transfer to a pestle and mortar and grind into a powder.

4. Heat 1 tbsp. of oil in a pan and cook the salad onions, add the garlic and cook for another few seconds. Then add the turmeric, ground fenugreek and cook for another minute. Tip the mixture in with the cooked potatoes. Add chopped coriander and mash together with a masher or fork.

5. Then shape into about 8-10 potato cakes, dust in flour and fry in the remaining oil for about 3-4 minutes until golden brown.

59

Dinner

I have tried to make the dinners interesting as well as added in some family favourites. The curry, stew and soup are all dishes with vegetable as the main ingredients, however they focus mainly on flavour. By adding the vegetables into a stew-like dish it takes the focus away from just eating a piece of broccoli into a more flavourful and exciting meal as a whole.

Avocado & Basil Pasta

Talk about a simple Pasta dish. Creamy avocado with creme fraiche and their favourite pasta, always a winner in our house.
And it can be enjoyed by the whole family.

Prep:5 Mins Cook: 12 mins for the pasta
Serves 2 adults and 2 kids

INGREDIENTS

1 ripe avocado
100ml crème fraiche
3 leaves of basil – chopped up finely
Juice of half a lemon
Parmesan cheese
1 cup of frozen peas and sweetcorn
225g pasta

METHOD

1. Boil the peas and corn for 3 or 4 mins.

2. Place the avocado, crème fraiche, basil, and lemon juice in a bowl and mash up to desired consistency.

3. Place the pasta in boiling water and cook according to the packet. Just before you drain the pasta take out a tablespoon of pasta water and add it to the avocado sauce.

4. Add the peas and corn and mix well.

5. Mix the pasta in with the sauce and sprinkle in the Parmesan cheese.

Butternut & Feta Cheese Frittata

I cut the butternut into large chunks but you can cut them smaller so that your baby is less likely to pick it out.

Serves: 8
Prep: 10 Cook: 20

INGREDIENTS

Half a butternut peeled and cut into small chunks
6 medium free-range eggs
2 garlic cloves
100g Greek feta cheese crumbled
1-tablespoon olive oil
1 onion
5 or 6 small potatoes – parboiled
50ml crème fraiche
Pepper to season

METHOD

1. Pre heat the oven to 180, fan 160.

2. Parboil the potatoes and butternut for about 5 mins.

3. Put the eggs, cheese, onion and garlic into a bowl. Mix and then add the pepper.

4. Heat the oil in a large frying pan (use one which is also suitable to use in an oven), pour the mixture into the pan and cook over a medium heat then scatter in the potatoes and butternut and cook for about 10 mins. Try not to move the mixture too much.

5. Transfer it to the oven and cook for a further 15-20 mins until golden brown.

6. Once it comes out of the oven, using a teaspoon dollop the crème fraiche randomly over the frittata creating pockets of crème fraiche in the frittata.

Baked Chicken Nuggets

What is it about chicken nuggets and kids!! I was adamant I didn't want my kids to touch them but I know when they get older they will find out about these things, so here's 'mums healthy nuggets'. Baked-not fried and covered in oats not breadcrumbs.
Result - Delicious. And another meal the whole family can enjoy.

Serves: 8-10 pieces
Prep: 15mins Cook: 30 mins

INGREDIENTS

4 chicken thighs
1 cup of oats
1 egg white - whisked
1⁄2 tsp cumin
1⁄2 tsp garlic powder

METHOD

1. Preheat the oven to 200, 180 fan.

2. In a shallow bowl add all the dry ingredients and mix.

3. In a separate bowl whisk the egg white.

4. Dip the chicken in the egg white, then the oat mixture and then place on a greased baking dish. Repeat for all four chicken pieces.

5. Bake for 30 mins and serve with my home-made baked beans and sweet potato wedges.

6. Cut the chicken from the bone for baby.

Creamed Spinach

This is a way of getting the iron rich spinach into their diet and do you know what...they love it! The butter and nutmeg take the mineral taste out and it can be poured over anything, I have blitzed it so that the texture is that of a puree. Drizzle over meat or fish or, as pictured, over fried hake and butternut.

Prep: 5 Cook: 5

INGREDIENTS

1/2 a bag of spinach
Knob of butter
1 small clove of garlic - crushed
1 shallot
25g fresh double cream
50ml full fat milk
Pinch of nutmeg for seasoning

METHOD

1. Heat the butter in a pan and brown off the shallot.

2. Add the garlic and cook for a further minute.

3. Add the chopped spinach and warm through.

4. Lastly add the milk and cream and cook until the spinach is fully wilted into the cream.

5. Season with nutmeg and then blitz with a food processor. Use this as a sauce for roasted vegetables.

Homemade Baked Beans

I put this recipe together as everyone loves baked beans on toast but they are full of sugar and salt and the reduced version is full of aspartame. This home-made baked bean recipe is healthier and just as tasty. I guarantee, you will not be disappointed, this family favourite tastes very similar to the version beginning with 'H', but better for you. You could scale up the quantity of ingredients to make a big bowl to last a few days

Prep: 5 mins Cook: 10 mins

INGREDIENTS

1x400g tin haricot beans
1 tbsp olive oil
1 small onion chopped finely
2 tbsp tomato puree
4 fresh tomatoes – chopped

METHOD

1. Drain the beans and place to one side.

2. Place the oil into a pan and add the onions. Cook them until they are soft adding the fresh tomatoes and the puree and cook for another 1-2 mins.

3. Place all of the ingredients apart from the beans into a food processor and blitz until smooth.

4. Place the tomato mixture and the beans in a pan together and mix, ensuring that all the beans are coated in the tomato sauce.

5. Cook through until warm. If you wish to eat the mixture at a later date you can reheat the bean mix.

Curried Lentils

As your baby becomes more adventurous in their eating you will probably find that they like highly flavoured foods. These curried lentils are a delicious side portion for grilled fish or chicken or eat them on their own as they are packed with protein.

Serves: 4
Prep: 10 mins Cook: 30 mins

INGREDIENTS

1 tbsp vegetable oil
1 medium onion, finely chopped
1 small carrot – diced
1 garlic clove – crushed
125g red lentils – rinsed
2 small potatoes – diced
1 tsp ground coriander
1 tsp ground cumin
1 tbsp tomato puree

METHOD

1. Heat the oil and fry off the onion and garlic until golden brown.

2. Add the spices and cook on a low heat for a minute.

3. Stir in the lentils, potatoes and carrot and tomato puree.

4. Then add about 400ml water. Bring to the boil and simmer covered for about 30 minutes. Stir occasionally to stop the lentils burning the bottom of the pan. Add more water if needed.

5. Serve once cooled or portion out and freeze for up to 1 month.

Fish Goujons

Every kid loves fish fingers, so I thought if they are going to be a regular then why not make my own. These fish goujons are also a great finger food for toddlers who are not quite using a knife and fork yet.

Makes: 6 goujons
Prep: 10 mins Cook: 5 mins

INGREDIENTS

2 fish fillets cut into sticks
1 egg, whisked
100g sesame seeds or almond flour
100g unsalted butter or coconut oil

METHOD

1. Set out the two bowls - one with the whisked egg and the other with the seeds or flour.

2. Heat the butter in a frying pan.

3. Quickly turn the fish sticks in the egg then in the sesame seeds or almond flour and fry for 3-5 minutes per side or until golden brown.

4. Serve with homemade baked beans and steamed or boiled sweet potato.

Ma's Tomato Food / Lamb Stew

My husband is from Cape Town and this is one of his family favourites. Its a great autumn or winter dish. Once you have blitzed the tomatoes there is not much else to do, so its a relatively easy stew to make also.

Prep: 30 mins Cook: 1 hour

INGREDIENTS
Lamb chops x 8
1 tbsp of vegetable oil
1kg ripe red tomatoes – blitzed
1 clove of garlic – crushed
1 onion
1 bay leaf
2 tbsp of tomato puree
3 small potatoes
1 tsp of tomato ketchup

INSTRUCTIONS

1. Firstly make sure you have liquidized all of the tomatoes and leave to one side.

2. Then heat the oil in a heavy bottomed saucepan over a medium to low heat.

3. Add the onions and brown off.

4. Add the meat and cook on a medium heat to brown. Add a little   water to stop the meat sticking or burning.

5. Add the tomatoes, tomato puree, garlic, bay leaf and tomato ketchup. Cook for 15 mins with the lid on.

6. Add the potatos and cook for about 12 to 15 mins.

7. To serve, make sure you remove the meat from the bones and cut up into bite size chunks for your little one

8. Serve with rice.

Quick Chicken Couscous with Roasted Veg

The simplicity of couscous makes it the perfect 'go-to' dish. OK, it can get messy with little ones, but they love it and you can serve it up with all sorts of vegetables.

INGREDIENTS

4 chicken thighs
3 tbsp oil
1 onion
1 small courgette
1 carrot
5 or 6 cloves garlic - whole
100g couscous

METHOD

1. Preheat the oven to 200/180 fan.

2. Quarter the onion, and roughly chop the veg ready for roasting. Place the veg in the oven and roast for 15-20 mins.

3. Meanwhile, heat one tablespoon of oil in the pan and shallow fry the chicken until golden brown.

4. Once the chicken and veg are done, pour around 150ml of boiled water over the couscous and cover. Leave to soak up the water for about 5 mins.

5. Then, using a fork, fluff up the couscous and add the roasted veg.

6. Chop up the veg further if you feel your baby needs smaller chunks.

7. Mix the couscous and veg together.

8. Chop up the chicken into bite size pieces and mix into the couscous mix.

Super Simple Carbonara

Its yummy and simple but needs to be eaten straight away. A great Sunday afternoon family lunch, when the kids have been playing in the garden all morning and need some carbs.

Serves: 2 kids portions

75g fusilli pasta
1 egg yolk
1 slice of good quality ham from outdoor-bred pigs
1/2 avocado sliced into small chunks
Small knob of butter

1. Put on a pot of water and bring to the boil. Cook the pasta according to the manufacturers instructions.

2. Meantime, separate an egg yolk from the white and place the yolk into a mixing bowl. Add some pepper and a small knob of butter. Whisk together.

3. Once the pasta is cooked, quickly drain it and then quickly add the egg mixture to the pasta and the heat of the pasta will cook the egg. You must be quick with this to ensure the heat is retained in the pot and the pasta. What I do is quickly drain the pasta, then throw it back into the pot and then add the mixture, add a splash (small splash) of water, give it a stir and put the lid on and shake it to ensure all the pasta is coated in the egg mixture. Add the torn up ham and the avocado and mix again.

4. Serve with some peas on the side or on its own.

One Pot Curried Fish and Rice

This is similar to Kedgeree. Whatever vegetables you have in the fridge, throw them in. This is such a simple but highly flavoursome dish.

Serves 2 adults and 2 kids
Cooking time 30 mins

INGREDIENTS
4 spring onions -trimmed and sliced
1tsp curry powder - mild or medium
1tsp fenugreek seeds
2 cloves of garlic - crushed
1tbsp vegetable oil
250g basmati
2 tomatoes - cut into small chunks
350g of any white fish, cut into chunks (you could use smoked fish also)
400g low salt stock - veg or fish

METHOD
1. Fry off the onion and garlic in the oil then add the spices, curry powder and Fenugreek seeds. Make sure you don't burn the spices so only cook them for 30 seconds or so.

2. Then add the tomatoes and cook for a further minute

3. Then add the fish and fry off for another 3 or four minutes just to get a bit of colour on the fish.

4. Add the rice and the stock. Bring to the biol and then reduce heat and simmer for around 20-25 minutes or until the rice is cooked and the stock is reduced fully.

Minestrone soup

I know...soup...are you mad!!! But trust me your kids will love it, if you drain off the liquid at first and serve them up the veg and pasta, it is soooo flavoursome they will forget they are eating veg. Then serve them up the liquor, for extra flavour and nutrients. They will have a full tummy and you will be very proud mum. Also this is another recipe that you can munch on for days.

Serves: 6-8
Prep Time: 30 mins – Cooking Time: 1 hour

INGREDIENTS
5 tbsp olive oil
2 onions
2 carrots
1 stick celery
1 tbsp. chopped sage
2 medium potatoes
2 leeks
1 can tomatoes or
6 fresh tomatoes, blitzed
1 large courgette
1 can of cannellini beans or chickpeas
3 pints of chicken or veg stock
1 pack of French beans
1 to 2 tablespoons of pesto (home made)
Parmesan to serve
Small pasta shapes – macaroni or similar

METHOD
1. In a very large saucepan heat the oil and sauté the onion, carrots, celery, sage until it begins to colour.

2. Then add the potatoes and leeks. Stir.

3. Add tomatoes, French beans and then the stock.

4. Bring to the boil then cover and simmer for about 1 hour.

5. Then add the chickpeas or cannellini beans. Add one can of water. And season with pepper. Bring back to the boil, add the pasta and cook for a further 15 mins or until the pasta is tender. Stir occasionally.

6. Finally add the pesto and serve with grated Parmesan (optional and mostly for you and not baby).

Mushroom Burgers

My kids love these – they are flavoursome and have just the right texture that they do not fall apart in their hands. Make all the mixture and you could make up actual burgers for the rest of the family. For the adults, add a brioche bun, lettuce, sliced beef tomato, a little ketchup and mayonnaise and you have a delicious veggie burger that is as satisfying as a beef burger.

Serves: 4
Cooking Time: 30 minutes

INGREDIENTS

1 tbsp. olive oil
250g pack of buttercup mushrooms
1 medium sized onion
2 clove of garlic
Small handful of spinach leaves
85g of breadcrumbs
400g can of chickpeas
Pinch of ground cumin
Pinch of ground coriander
Pinch of mild curry powder (optional)
Juice of half a lemon

METHOD

1. Heat the oil in a non-stick frying pan.
2. Add the mushrooms and onion and garlic and spinach until the spinach is completely wilted.
3. Add the spices and the lemon juice
4. Drain the chickpeas and mash them up with a fork thoroughly
5. Add the mushroom mixture into the chickpeas.
6. Add the breadcrumbs
7. Mix with your hands until all the mixture is combined. Shape into patties the desired shape and size.
8. Fry in a little oil for 3 -4 mins each side or until browned and crisp
9. Serve with either hummus/yoghurt and cucumber

Sardines and Pasta

Depending on who eats this you might have quite a lot of sauce so you could put some in the fridge and serve for the next day or use the sauce for a family meal.

Serves: 2 adults and 2 kids
Prep Time: 5 – Cooking Time: 15

INGREDIENTS

1 can of sardines in tomato sauce
1 can of chopped tomatoes
1 small onion - chopped up finely
1 garlic clove - crushed
200g pasta

METHOD

1. Fry off the onion in a little olive oil, add the garlic, then the tomatoes and cook for a further minute.

2. Finally add the sardines and warm through.

3. Cook your pasta and then mix the sauce and pasta together.

Shepherds Pie with Cauliflower Mash

This comfort food is lovely made with lamb or you could use Quorn as a veggie alternative. Make it with minced beef and you have a cottage pie!

INGREDIENTS

Nob of unsalted butter
1 pack or approx. 400g of minced beef or lamb
1 onion
1 large carrot
3 or 4 mushrooms
1 garlic clove – crushed
6 fresh tomatoes – blitzed
1 tbsp tomato puree

For the topping:
1 whole cauliflower broken into florets
1 small parsnip – peeled and chopped into small pieces
A knob of unsalted butter
150g grated cheddar cheese
A few sprigs of flat leaf parsley, chopped

METHOD

1. Preheat the oven to 180/160 fan..

2. Heat the butter in a pan then fry the mince until brown. Add onion and fry off until translucent. Add the vegetables, chop them up into small pieces before adding them to the pan. Add the puree and blitzed up tomatoes. Cook for about 10 mins. If mixture dries out add water.

3. Meanwhile, boil the cauliflower and parsnip for about 5-6 mins. Once cooked, mash together with the butter and cheese.

4. Place the meat mixture in a over proof dish and make sure the whole bottom is covered, then add the cauliflower mixture and spread over in a layer covering all the meat mixture.

5. Add the parsley and cook in the oven for about 20-30 mins.

Super Healthy Potato Salad
Made with Yoghurt

By substituting yoghurt for mayonnaise you are left with a much more refreshing and healthy potato salad for the whole family.

Serves 4
Prep and cook time 15 mins

8-10 small potatoes
3 large tbsp. of live natural runny
yoghurt
1tsp of capers
1/2tsp of French mustard
3 spring onions – finely chopped
1 garlic clove crushed
1 hard-boiled egg
Pepper to season

METHOD

1. Boil the potatoes and egg (throw the egg in at the last five mins of boiling the potatoes)

2. Make the dressing – mix the yoghurt, mustard, garlic, spring onion, capers and pepper in a mixing bowl.

3. Once potatoes and egg are cooked. Peel the egg and let them cool 95%. Grate the egg into to mixture and add the potatoes and stir until all potatoes are coated in the mixture.

Super Simple Vegetable Curry
with Coconut Milk

I know what your thinking – curry for babies! And you are also thinking, when the heck am I going to have the time to make a curry. Well this curry is not hot firstly, and secondly it is so simple you will have it cooked up in less than half an hour, trust me:) Also your little ones will love it; its very flavoursome.

Prep: 15 mins Cook: 30 mins

INGREDIENTS

1/2 butternut
1 onion
2 garlic cloves
4/5 small salad potatoes
1 large bunch of green beans
400g can of coconut milk

1/2 tsp. turmeric
1 tsp. fenugreek seeds
1 stick of cinnamon
1 kefir lime leaf
Pepper to taste
Rice to serve

METHOD

1. Chop up the butternut and potato into 2cm cubes and leave to one side.

2. Heat the oil in a pan and gently fry the onion and cinnamon stick until soft.

3. Add the garlic turmeric and fenugreek seeds and stir for one minute making sure not to burn the spices.

4. Add the butternut, potato and green beans and stir for a further minute.

5. Add the kefir leaves, coconut milk and 150ml water. Bring to the boil and then lower the heat and simmer, covered for about 15-20 mins. Checking on the potato and butternut.

6. Serve with rice.

Super Easy Fish Pie

Fish pie without the faff! No rue, no complicated cooking processes and still delicious!

Prep: 15 mins Cook: 15 mins

INGREDIENTS

1 pack of fish pie mix
300ml of whole milk
75g frozen peas
Pinch of pepper
75g medium or mature cheddar cheese
3 or 4 small potatoes – cut up into quarters
Knob of butter

METHOD

1. Preheat oven to 200/180 Fan.

2. Boil the potatoes then drain.

3. Pour the milk into a saucepan. Pop in the fish and then turn on the heat and start to simmer the fish in order to poach it for about 7-8 minutes or until the fish flakes easily.

4. Whilst the fish is poaching, steam/boil the peas of 2 minutes and then set aside.

5. Once the fish is poached pour some of the milk into the pot of potatoes and add a knob of butter and grate the cheese in. Mash the potato mix until smooth.

6. Place the fish into an oven proof dish pour in some of the milk and pour in the peas. Then add the mashed potato and even out the mixture to cover the fish.

7. Bake for 10-15 mins.

PARTY SNACKS

Add the personal touch to their birthday. I have tried to keep the sugar levels down without compromising on flavour. The older kids will also enjoy the recipes.

It's a time to celebrate without peeling your kids off the walls with a sugar high!

Try out my oat crusted chicken nuggets (pg 66) or my fish goujons (p.g 72) and potato wedges (p.g 44)

Buffet Ideas for a Birthday party

Corn on the cob

Simply boil the corn on the cob for 6-7 minutes and roll in butter straight afterwards.

Roasted mandolin potatoes

Using a thickest slice option on the mandolin - slice the potatoes, drizzle a little oil and pepper and pop in a hot oven for 30-40 minutes. They come out like crisps.

Tortilla bread with hummus rolled up

Cover the tortilla with butter and hummus - roll up into a long cigar and cut into 1 inch pieces.

Apple with peanut butter dip

Simply slice an apple into wedges and serve with peanut butter that's been thinned out with any non diary milk. I use almond as its slightly sweet.

Sliced avocado and melted cheese strips

Slice thick strips of cheddar cheese and grill on baking paper until melted(watch the paper doesn't catch the grill!). Once they cool the cheese will harden and you can peel off and serve with sliced avocado.

Kebabs

Try sausage or tofu, cherry tomatoes and yellow pepper. Use the wooden lolly sticks with the rounded edge to be safe though.

Banana & Blueberry Sugar Free Muffins

You will not believe these have absolutely no sugar in them. They don't crumble too much and your kids will love them.

Serves: 12
Prep:10 Cook: 20

INGREDIENTS

225g mashed banana
1 egg
125ml water
125ml vegetable oil
250g wholemeal flour
1tsp bicarb of soda
2 tsp baking powder
150g fresh or frozen blueberries

METHOD

1. Preheat the oven to 180/gas mark 4. Grease 12 muffin cups or line with paper muffin cases.

2. Mix together the mashed bananas, egg, water and oil in a large bowl.

3. Mix in the flour, bicarb and baking powder until mostly smooth.

4. Gently fold the blueberries into the mixture.

5. Bake for about 20 minutes or until the tops spring back when pressed.

Fruit Yoghurt Lollipops

No sugar - no additives - they look fabulous - and kids love to get to the fruit bit inside.

Serves: 8
Prep Time: 10 minutes

INGREDIENTS

1.5 cups of natural live yoghurt
1tbsp of agave syrup
1.5 cup of frozen berries
2-3 tbsp chopped hazelnuts for the tips of the
lollies or chocolate sprinkles or desiccated coconut

INSTRUCTIONS

1. Sprinkle the topping (I am using chopped nuts) into the lolly holders.

2. Then mix the yoghurt, berries and Agave syrup together in a mixing bowl then spoon the mixture into the lolly moulds and stick the spoon in.

3. Put in the freezer preferably over night to freeze.

NOTE;
You will need lolly holders for these and I used the boys spoons as the holders as they are easier to grip.

Watermelon Cake

Whoever came up with this idea is a genius! It looks like a red velvet cake but its actually watermelon, kids love it and adults even more. Perfect party food, espesially for summer babies, and it won't leave you peeling them off the walls with a sugar fix.

INGREDIENTS

1 medium watermelon
300-500ml double cream – whipped to thick peaks
Mixed berries or soft fruit of your choice

METHOD

1. Slice off the top and bottom of the watermelon skin then cut away the rest of the skin to create a cake like shape.
2. Cover the cake with the cream and then decorate with the fruit.

Chocolate Covered Banana Lollies

These are fab for kids birthday parties and a secret way of getting fruit into them. Also they are so easy, you could prep these the night before. Use a good quality chocolate.

Prep: 5 mins

INGREDIENTS

1/2 Banana
Chocolate - melted
nuts, fruit, seeds, coconut

METHOD

1. Cut a banana in half

2. Dunk it in a bowl of melted chocolate (use a bain-marie; saucepan of water and a bowl of chocolate placed over the top), be quick otherwise the chocolate will harden.

3. Then roll in nuts, fruit, seeds, coconut, hundreds and thousands etc..

4. Leave to cool on greaseproof paper.

Index

Fish and rice, one pot dish, 78
Fish pie, 91
Fish, and sweet potato puree, 19
Flour and yoghurt flatbreads, 48
Frittata, butternut and feta, 64
Fritters, Sweetcorn, 50
Fruit yoghurt lollipops, 96

Gails sweetcorn fritters, 50
Gemma's porridge loaf, 53
Gluten free pizza, 55
Granola, 32

Hummus, beetroot, 41
Hummus, original, 44

Lamb stew, 74

Minestrone Soup, 80
Mushroom burgers, 82
Oat flapjacks, 34
Oat, Gemma's porridge loaf, 53
Onion bahji, 56

Pasta, pesto and pine nuts, 52
Pea puree, 21
Pear puree, 21
Potato cakes, 46
Potato salad, 88
Potato, leek and pea puree, 22

Rissoles, 40

Sardines and pasta, 84
Savoury muffin's, 58
Shepherds pie, 86
Sweet potato puree, 23
Sweet potato wedges, 44
Sweetcorn, fritters, 50

Watermelon cake, 98

MILLILITRES	TEASPOONS
2ml	1/4 tsp
3ml	1/2 tsp
5ml	1 tsp
10ml	2 tsp
20ml	4 tsp

MILLILITRES	TABLESPOONS
15ml	1 tbsp
30ml	2 tbsp
45ml	3 tbsp

MILLILITRES	CUPS	GRAMS*
60ml	1/4 cup	31g
80ml	1/3 cup	42g
125ml	1/2 cup	63g
160ml	2/3 cup	83g
200ml	3/4 cup	94g
250ml	1 cup	125g
375ml	1 1/2 cups	188g
500ml	2 cups	250g
1 litre	4 cups	500g

*Please note that these conversions are approximations based on dry ingredients i.e flour and should only be taken as a guide

Bibliography

1. The Flavour Led Weaning cookbook by Zainab Jagot Ahmed. Published by Ebury Press

2. Baby Food Matters by Dr Clare Llewellyn and Dr Hayley Syrad. Published by Yellow Kite

3. Feeding your baby and toddler from first foods to family meals - Annabel Karmel. Published by Dorling Kindersley ltd.

4. Healthy Food for Healthy baby - Monique Le Roux Forslund. Published by Struik Lifestyle.

Lightning Source UK Ltd.
Milton Keynes UK
UKHW020623141118
332316UK00009B/166/P